THE NINETEENTH CENTURY AND OTHER POEMS

THE NINETEENTH CENTURY AND OTHER POEMS
ISBN 978-0-9773401-5-6

Design by Zach Barocas
Cover photograph by Peter O'Leary

For permission to reprint more than several lines
of this book or for other inquiry, please write to
THE CULTURAL SOCIETY
culturalsociety.org | publisher@culturalsociety.org

Grateful acknowledgement is made to the editors and staffs
of the following publications in which some of these poems first appeared:
Dislocate, *Fifth Wednesday*, *The Literary Review*, *Milk*, *Zoland Poetry*.
Many thanks to David Pavelich and Answer Tag Home Press.

"The Nineteenth Century" is dedicated to Ralph Johnson.

"Byzantine Ode" is dedicated to Joel Craig.

Thanks also to Peter O'Leary, for helping this book discover its shape;
to the Hair Club and Bazaar; to Devin King; and always, to Jennifer Rupert.

Italicized portions of some of the prose passages in
"An Archive of a Work-in-Progress" quote
William Carlos Williams' KORA IN HELL.

THE NINETEENTH CENTURY
AND OTHER POEMS BY CHRIS GLOMSKI

THE CULTURAL SOCIETY
BROOKLYN MMXI

CONTENTS

TO THE READER (FARROW)

You lack charm   And yet
I find you charming   Your
olfactory organ does not lend
characterization
a hog nose and that's
saying something   Or there's
asking as in do you find me
charming too   Of course
you do it's what I
demand of you
simply by leaving you
out   Though now it would
appear that I lack
you   Much as I like you

Masked by the wheels of umbrellas the private faces flash. A primitive billboard's conceptual flower it's morning. Soda rinsed against the blind metaphysic of rails good luck hanging a new sky

Too much not enough in advance. Pointillist implosions. Sunday afternoon spent revolutionizing the swan boat of cannibal economies based on pineapples and sugar

Japan Jena Jesuit Johannes. Maria Marten in the red barn at Polsted Containing the whole Account of the horrid Murder. It happens the governor was accustomed to walk at that hour. Tripped on my way to Soho and thieves were all over me

More mysteriously, Franz Liszt. Paris barricades. Contemplating the domestic atmosphere from the little house outside. The banker was apparently suffering from dropsy and resembled a Pre-Raphaelite manuscript interred with a bier. Retrieved later by the banker's friends

Fango è il mondo. Malaria insufficiently reported by press. Where do we come from? Where are we going? To locate the source of the Nile. Every morning and night, I've always been praying that I and my whole regiment may soon be called to do it, and that we may do it absolutely well and proper

Away to Montevideo to the colonies of waterproof carpets maps tents the red velvet of the tongues of fleas draining the marshes' cattails of furniture ensembles devised for therapeutic purposes, galvanic columns of dark bodies the wings of electric labor forming oppressive glottals on whose river memory flows like spittle rushed by the wind's empirical crash through a hurricane of unacceptably profound stillness like lashes on the M of Martinique

Attacks of kleptomania brought on by elevators and menswear. A salon painting hung in a certain saloon. Receding in multiple eyes. Nebular thrill of the arcades

Afternoons alone in the salon studying paintings of a certain saloon. Last week I witnessed a skater stoop, without stopping, to sweep a woman's glove. Several nights now dreaming of roly-polying in its creases. Would go to see that doctor but have already forgotten his name

Cattle from the western states go east by rail. Grant enduring his two terms. "Us" is not "them," though in general both we and they build a bridge. 1899: a new crane swings over the marsh in our sky

Calligraphic shadow of the Ripper behind a Japanese screen. Mary H found it presently profitable to become a governess in a noble family. Leaves lean into the wind with broad gestures

Malthusian devil unleashed, London, Paris, NYC. The clock unleashes an automatic machinery, a new rhythm, and it's time for work

The electric eel up to 550 volts through the water you become a bronze statue in flames beneath wires of sunset. If in Debussy the nerves are elided with the sound of music, silence is mechanized. Silence is acoustic

Eternal material slag-heap of changing seasons, boots and colors. No way to divide the discus of being thrown by this endlessly playing record

JUST THE THING

would be
a book
on which the rain
fell voluptuously
as in
IL PLEUT
the cover painted
profile of
Apollinaire
avec pipe   Above
it things taped to
the wall the better
to remember   An old
Halloween mask
mouth brow and eyes
painted on *jutte*
in post-impressionist aux-
Ypsilanti-Michigan style
Not a lotta news
beyond this winter
weather   Count on
clearing the car of
pillowy tufts, then deciding
to take the train   Cough
It's crowded, too many
books on this desk   Define
'Rockist' as one
who thinks Iggy
still looks good with-
out a shirt   The verb is
always tense   It should relax,
take off its shirt!   It's chafing my
hands, it's the dry air
the arctic chill, did you
get some more Lubriderm?

The catfish swivels his
eyes at the bottom of the
aquarium Or hers Also on
the wall a work on
cardboard by Jake
Smith 'sends in its turn the
needed rain' Somewhere the sun
is setting behind a leafy forest
overlooking the sea Not here
It's night and the bathtub
was an ice bucket until I
could get heat flowing
through showerhead
shivering then dialing back
on the too-hot stream In Italy
caldo sounds a little like *cold*
until experience associates
with scald-o and scalding is
a better word than too-hot
to describe water that
spills from a pan
dragged from stove
by a curious tot About the likeness
of infinite cold to infinite
heat A boreal
poet *skalds* like the Norse
aurora Back to basics Dr. Jkl;
Mr. Qwert Trees Pictures
of trees hung
above a closet
whose sliding
door reveals a paint chip
in outline of South America
where blazes currently
the beautiful gas jet

of summer   Having
a great time   Wish you
were   The departed
placed in frames   The milk
crate on the floor   Streetlamp
spills on carpet   The independently
declared being of things
beyond Tuesday   A literal
figure assembled in
time   For what   For
metaphor   The former tree
ornament now the cat's
toy   Holiday as
photographed blur   Used
with "the" to indicate the
proper or fashionable
way things nudge against
other things   Hence
paper writes on pen   Is
then cremated by computer
Or is lost within key-
board   The paint dried
in varicose drips   This
swivel chair contains
an I   Am he   Eh   Amo
not sufficiently preferred
to ammo   And loving hooks
its phantom sign   No one
will know I'm speaking
to you   No one will think
I am speaking   No one
will know that no one will think
I am speaking

TRANSFORMATIONS

If chance
is the bottle imp
of every inquiry inside one, if one
hacks peg leg from living wood
and sinks into sand the scorpions rub,
if one is staring and that way stung, if one
becomes a tenant inside a scent that isn't

If you tithe your clearest thinking with clinamen
you strayed from, if you con some useless instruction
to which entropy is haltered,
if you are spurred
by convictions that you
aren't, if so deterred
you scant what is...

MAPPING A BLIND SPOT

Emptying the pulse
of its strange information into
presence keyed on
the air, immaculate vestibule
into which an envelope falls
through the slot of the other
hemisphere, where you recognize
your own fingers prying
open this fatal radius of a
cartographer's dream, unfolding it
over all the old familiar places

ANNUAL

A few minutes come to life, though that was long ago, and all that time
    no one mentioned it.
Now the minutiae languish in junk drawers, invisible until reclaimed
    or willed unintentionally
Away. Still, they have never been more surrounded by what spreads;
    it is not an illusion; it
occurs where their ranks concretize abstractions, sky
    and polar cap, reflected on
The water. If you were influenced by anything, it was less the dive's degree
    of difficulty than the foresight
Of having cameras there. As if you both did and did not believe it.
The banter was condensed as others regarded you through
    acknowledged routines, which while
Seldom tallying toward the scrutable, somehow managed to drag us from the
    mat of common sense where we had found it
Hard to work. But why are there always a bunch of flowers standing in the way?
And what are they there for if not to remind us of sex and other behaviors
    according to which people get touchy? As balm lulls
The bee, the day hulls into evening; cars skidding home
    in sudden but expected rain as if
At sea, abandoning accustomed sounds. Splash of appointments
    skipped like stones across a series
Of follow-ups; indifferent, uncited hours that take place between
    talking to others and to oneself as to
Any arbitrary, though hardly neutral, audience. Then something crashes
    in the middle. Night's seams
Deepen beneath more rain and more thunder, like a cradle. Mushrooms
    prompted by a damp upward sense
Of this late day blazing like the Dogstar, and echoed
    in wings whose appearance is sudden and brief,
Signifying the presence of an end. It is that it is what, if not important to be
    held accountable for how one thing is not
Like any other, until suddenly, in eminent difference, it is? Things take up the
    crouch of their appearance, or do you mean crutch? These

Questions construct a kind of awkward infinity, unending in its shyness, a
nervous prolonging, remarkable for having shown up.
Still talking about the same things, still guided by shades of a fauve-like
appetite; singular in its purpose, it
Dislodges an alternate view of yourself. Hence it appears that we are
waiting again for something to recall
Truly: how misshapen the continent looked, the pluses and minuses in an airport
mosaic, brief flutterings, petals, an eye.
And if there is fuzziness in these spaces set before you, at least their terminus is
as abrupt as whatever grows shorter, having lengthened
Accordingly, the day it was around us.

AN IDEA

Is phantom form   A quantity
of minutes following
a checked bid to
place the afternoon
here   To be
continued or carried
in one's pocket   If the
idea is to win something
decisive or as definite
as the line
between then and
now   To be even   Or as
unfinished, as mythical as
shipwrecks punctuated
by the cool depths of
their interiors   To be
ridden out   On
the axle of the phrasal
the dream of the scoured
parking lot turns
on a genuine anguish
for the missing car   Pointed
toward some indefinite
quality   The fulcrum of
'An Idea'   Which is
a poem begun yesterday   Meant
to finish the afternoon   Eidolon
of other time   Away where
we may drive
that car

A STORY

When narrative reveres its constant stream
refrain for a time from conceiving
"in the hip pocket of a thing that's done"

When narrative reveres its constant stream,
whose summer thought, grown gold in autumn,
withdraws onto a terrace, muttering things?

When narrative reveres its constant stream
refrain for a time from conceiving

INFINITY

after Giacomo Leopardi

A vague forest blooms where there is room
tendrilling through our need for a hedge

To fathom the cleaving, to sink and become
a vague forest blooming where there is room
a thought must twist and lift, and then succumb,
falling back upon the knife's edge

A vague forest blooms where there is room
tendrilling through our need for a hedge

SPECULAR SEQUENCE

1

“Gonna see what my little mind
can”   Then sleep
through whatever you say
when fumbling with the alarm   Snow
falling like asterisks   Who said we never enter
alone

2

Bad Capitol example   Only imagine
they’re hearing it with more than perfunctory
feeling   More than a usual mix of scripted
footsteps on stair or the echo of calling
down to them   Did you remember milk   No but you
slipped on the sidewalk or something obvious like
that   Or snow falls and the inner
glow can’t keep up with it   And the object
of the morning is tossed aside   Falls
to be continued

3

Coldness of insight war and world   Which is
what peace be to you   Hung
without its original sense and limited to type   Barred
by font   Revolutionary circle of your
preposition   Stitch stick snitch sounding out your
Saxon   The rhyme will need some floral snare   Saxifrage
or abandon

4

Specular horses advance in your eye   Finding
a willow there or plume of water bent
to breeze across the angered scent of
that excitement

5

This is getting good   That is the
getting   Here deathshead here kitty   Believe
my balm if you've the room   If by days
we attune our schedule to
the serious glance   Given
pause   Given clause   Now get

6

And then   And then if there
slips through this   This
discontinuity   Pieces of it
puzzle   T for instance   Or the
eye is his type   To bite or else
swirl through fine dust in January's
closet   The newer years tickering right
to left or left ticking right   Our two-faced
reading of time   And temper   Full
of in-betweenness you just keep going
till things arrive stamped with a new
address

BYZANTINE ODE

after John Ash

It was already the landscape of the future   A
place to leave but which will drift like a phosphene
slowly back across your sight   Cattails in the world's
largest industrial park where cyclists leaned
hard in the turns of Sunday races   They loved the empty
spaces and seemed to bring them back to earth   Revived
on screen they grew taller against the blur of the river
that is not a river (though we might ask where it is taking
us)   And our days are calm and numbered in the mirrors
of Jewels   In the valleys of lights   It's all very
queer how high the planters rise   How needless
intensifiers succor the aisles of coffee

                                                            you are invisible
again   Oblivion is both eager and a baroque instrument
one holds up to one's neck   And if one's neck becomes
a Doric column around which leaves blow in the sunlight
what kind of a staircase could circle that   And who
would you impose upon to climb it as far as the water
tank of your thoughts spray-painted CLASS OF '84   These
and certain other periods are missing in the names
of our desire   Neglected not by any night so much as
betrayed by its location   A tall figure pedaling through
the empty park enters tennis court and lobs an oath
across the net   For a moment you are free on this island
of vagrant passes to handle that moment slowly

                                            one need never leave the greenery
to enjoy one's confines   Having drowned in our cars we are
alive there in the manner of travelers returning
though it is difficult not to be menaced by that air   Comes
suddenly a shadow crossing the valley   In the evening
they attend to the cooking   *How* we also wonder *does*
the end of summer emerge   Is it always preceded by

gatherings around physical graffiti
underneath the bridge   Something in the way   And yet
these somethings linger on almost as if you'd
asked them to

                                        the title so irresistibly splendid
we die intensified by histories which needn't be
discarded as a complete sham for having been
drawn through men of women or men through them   Clio's
father *in an onslaught against fun booby-trapped*
the banisters she loved to slide down   Kings turn
up dead in history's hand and children flock to social
networks racing greenly in the stretch   Who's
read there floats to the surface   And so it can take
years to decipher the burned pages scattered in back
of one's skull   Or the mummy's two thousand years
embedded within   Mixes present with past whose
music just happens to pass down the same street
as you

                                names
remain obdurate
fixtures   Who would we be having succumbed
to every desire to change them   Committed
to their pages memory will reinvent a new
type of S   Or C   I remember the first time I was alone
with Circe   She cupped my chin as I lay
in my bunk   A new and intolerable language
whirred in my throat   In service to the spoke
blurring the air

IL PLEUT

The sentence begins the sentence began by thinking
Of rain as something it was no longer saying, sluiced

Through its syntax and from which meaning
Would be duly sifted. Summer threw its weight

On the pavement, as strollers came and went all
Hours, brisk at the corners. Night wore a wig of colored lights.

Still, the blank expressions, the debris of festival seating
Trailed like breadcrumbs through a new library

Everyone's doing research in. It's raining, someone maintains.
They'll say it for the first time if you ask them to repeat it.

IL NE PLEUT PAS

The sentence began "the sentence began," having ushered
Us guests into its way of speaking. And yet we still

Will have to wait for the light and cross within white lines
Reflected on dark pavement inside us, etched in deference

Not to anarchy, but evening. The traffic cop gets all leonine, seething.
We're pedestrian to the cyclists pedaling by.

A river runs through shores of which the street reminds us.
Each image streams through the others and even manages

To seem uplifting, though we're less inclined to read
into so many near misses a plausible ending.

SPIRITS

Someone you know
has died
and that distance peals Styro-
foam and plastic mixed
with papery sycamore
leaves and spring pounces
a blue pulp
behind his
knees   The surface
crackles   One
adjusts the picture   Extends
an arm toward evening   It's
raining and your face is
paper   An odd double
descending a staircase
of letters   Skeletal hand over
skeletal motion unfolding   The
words pressed in the
banister   Don't think
just hold the article
in place of something more
definite the bare
beginning still a long way
off in this improv
of sudden
crocuses up
from the mud   The
operational
wind   A telephone
ringing elsewhere   Yet
gladdened by absence
within the particular
you are specific enough
to shine like bronze   Clash

of silverware tossed in
plastic compartments   A blue
dais of late March drains as
such in swished liqueur   If
too much time has passed
it's early   Chronology
encounters turbulence
in wormholes
in a garden where the rain
filters through   You are struck by
the random perception   Time
of an inexhaustible place
where you are forbidden
to go inside you   Every-
thing and nothing to do
with death shining in
the long lashes of
squinting pleasurably into
it   The tug of something
unseen reeled to creek's
surface   Sunlit immeas-
urably free and worth
drowning for

IT'S NOT WHAT YOU THINK IT IS

There is a place for it Even if
only tagging along It will
emerge to render its preface
transparent It's in possession
of the kingdom Breaking
into blossom it will build
its threshold on sight Now
it's listening and
marked by a kind
of velvet eruption The
cling of it is meant
to ward off evil Yet evil
flourishes around it It snows
in some tulips to inhabit
what no one hears There
was a time when it
was carried by freshets
on the Little Miami
which isn't where you'd think
it is Mere geography's
not it Sometimes it
confuses the cursor with I
who stand
around blinking as if
at some remove
from things that falter That's
not it nor is it helped
to more than a blindfold
a personification Once it
is down to a single string there
is really no sort of question you
can put to it It seeks its
own kind Crying like a dog It's

10 o'clock at night   It is a dog   It's not
mine   It lives two doors
away   Tomorrow it may
change its tune the way it does
when another dog walks
by   A female dog is not
a doe   A deer is not
blue   True or false   It's a trick
question   Read it for what
it's worth   There are many deer
outside Reading, Pennsylvania beneath
the pines at dusk   As if outside reading
its first intensity flared   Then faltered
in its aura of absence   Or so it
is written

THE BANGS

after Eugenio Montale

"You mustn't" or "don't" is only an attack
which covers you   Veiled by puerile
distractions   Or dangled like the little ankhs
on your lobes   My hand shouldn't touch
them as if they were adjuncts to some
solar pulse   Accelerated and
untucked by words that are
themselves asleep   Swans
haunt the lunatic wherever you wake
distended with forgiveness toward
such stillborn wings that neither can
confuse the dawn, nor leap from
its heights to hide it

POEM

Then mention rain again
to help rewind its undulant
sound around the wheels

(or wheels of thought) waking
to wet pavement outside. An *I am*
isn't anything,

a means to skip a beat
or leave a bleeding valentine
balled up like a hit-and-run

struck down beside the road.
Then mention rain falling upon
the dunes again. It helps

deliver evening to
the ragged boys who caroled in
that rain, who swam beyond

the ragged buoys bouncing in the surf.

ON "THE LIBRARIAN" BY CHARLES OLSON

for David Pavelich

The landscape always
already parenthetical   Away
from the queue of waves
tipping onto shore   And yet
maximal objects
mostly recede within
the eye and often
flee the mind   Harvested
from leaden
words, they
lend themselves to
stacks one browses
in hope they'll
return as something
else   A hollowed
hardcover with oiled impression
of revolver   See who is
more frank once the
questioning begins

RECONSTRUCTED FABLE

Facies hippocratica disclosing notes
        it beats from the harmonic whole
Addressing every none-in-particular
Animated rooftop blushed in dead aim waves
        thus imperfectly remembered.
I is for illusion, there is a place and time for anything
        that entrances the teacup floating
In your eye. You keep it hooked upon a finger
        of ordinary elapsement, remembered
As an ordinary day, t-shirt soaked from no strain
        greater than walking to the cleaner's
Which you don't often use (though there it's fun to observe
        those I imagine do). Did I say "I" when
I meant "you"? Chalk it up to this lemony light
        or the wreathy smoke of wishful thinking.
Blue smoke curtains sucked into window,
Quieted cicadas still in ear, the buzz of shoulders
        a fan trains cool air on.
The sun wilts marigolds planted in Clementine
        crates. I finish reading *Locus Solus*, it ends
Matter-of-factly, I rummage for the watering can. It's great
To be able to do things, pouring out a cool drink of life
        or installing implements of order
Like the workers I saw yesterday unloading incomprehensible
        objects from a green horse trailer,
In and out of which these were heaped and spilling and I
        could not for the life of me grasp
What they were. As I drew closer I recognized
        proportions and at the same time didn't.
They were grounded traffic lights, so much bigger than
        they seem hanging in air. That moment's
Poe-like transformation brings me back a tiny
        kind of aphid I watched in last year's
Garden, bloodstone and lapis markings like a jeweled
        Egyptian beetle's. Imagine

its presence magnified, as in a movie,
Twenty-thousand times; if one had to live that movie,
would beauty change immediately
To terror? Most of what's around seems to change more
slowly, like red to green, if one is
In a hurry. The light changes and men in yellow helmets change
the lights. How will traffic signals
Of the future look? Probably not much different,
but I seem to remember, when Jen first
Moved to Wicker Park, the lights at Division and Damen were perched
rigid and low on strictly vertical posts, not
Yet overhanging the intersection. Best of all were diminutive lights
reading STOP and GO for crossing pedestrians.
"It's a shame," we said, when change was imminent,
"those will have to go." Till now,
I'd forgotten them with the aphid. Soil for the garden. It isn't
easy remembering things, especially
When heat indices file so many in the Midwest under "July,
those who were cooked in."
Several articles in today's *Sun-Times* address
the weather, one of the few things we all
Share. The phatic is like a secret virgin grossly
shared by many mouths! What would
Sister Addolorata say? I need a cool drink, maybe
a Classic Coke. You can't get
Fresca anymore, was that bottled by Coke? If you
visit Florence, ask for "Hoha-Hola."
Dry clouds pass over the reservoir of night.
Our inward songs continue, repeated repeatedly,
a cricket sheen to cozen sleep
Where snake-like creatures slither toward you and —
stepped on — somehow bleed like glass
Breaks. When I read this morning that Tropical Storm
Chris was "gaining in strength"

I was secretly pleased. But time passes and one rebuilds,
as my memory has rebuilt
Around the fact I never checked to learn what became of us,
though I meant to see if we'd
Wreaked some Eastern seaboard havoc, but not such as
wrecked New Orleans, city I have most
Wanted to see, and most have not.
August delusions
of the delta steeping in the Gulf,
Southeast of Breton Sound. And there is Lake Pontchartrain,
turbid and menacing below its causeway.
Between these waters lies the city whose name rolls off
its citizens' tongues
In so many surprising ways! They've been evacuated from
Lakeview and its promise of "coastal living
Only a short ride from downtown." No sailboats
on the lake today on account
Of these low and rotating clouds. It is a Monday morning,
and we'd hoped to see
Fishermen casting from the levees for flounder, but instead
we are moved to climb the higher ground
Of Gentilly, whose moss-green bungalows and English cottages
are mostly boarded up.
There's no one around, so it seems we have the run
of several vine-laced gardens.
What a strange thrill to be here, gazing inside walls
which in an ordinary year
Would serve to shut us out. What harm in picking from
the hoards of magenta flowers? Or does
This thrill spring from a sense that something bigger may be
looking back at us?

Carla, Betsy, Camille, Hugo,
Fran, Katrina, Audrey, Opal, Wilma, Ike — the halcyon
instant quivers in your
Eyes. And who are we to demand, "Excuse us, could you
point the way to Musician's Village?"
Here in a stranger's garden, our guidebook comes to resemble
a fictional work we will ourselves
To believe in. Does Marigny, "the plantation
of a Creole bon vivant who made
Dice games popular in America," even exist? The French
Quarter seems more like an idea
Than an inevitability of intimate sidewalks and houses
colored red, yellow, green.
And that aphid's belly looms hideous overhead, tumid
with the devoured leaves of
All our former dancing days.

New Orleans, hello
and goodbye. July calls again, but it is
Not the same July: Dear Chris, hello. Some of your
prose paragraphs echo KORA IN HELL,
But that's ok. How strange to be three years
in three years
Gone. No man that has not gathered / The sprig of gold
is given leave to penetrate / The hidden world
Beneath the mortal one. The dunes in Gary are scary
accurate, as when, just as, so it is about
Ninety minutes ago the rain fell in literal *sheets*, rain-covers
of sheer density, landing in thick
horizontal blankets, like a sequence of
Counterpanes spread one on top of another.

The pitcher throws a "slurve" and angers
the spell-check. Checked by the spell of a gondola
Taken to the top of a ski-run in July, the blur of the run
in its meadow phase, impastoed with pinks
And yellows, scarlets and blues. I think I'm getting the flu,
"up the Mississippi and into
the Great Lakes."

Vacant lot Damen and Lake rank with chicory,
Queen Anne's lace. It is time for the destruction of error, is it?
If not we must build around it, making notes
On sincerity. It was Easter as I was raking in July.
You see another skull inside distant
Wasted days soon to die. Out-of-sorts odysseys turn
us back on love of average height
And average build. Then went down to the shapes again
and held the man for nothing — Some bashful
Summer's Day — Down among the ships, having hosted
six gold parties these last six months,
I took the total tone of infra-red inscriptions below. As the
fireworks broke open the sky,
Stark horses peered over their stalls. John Henry,
Eight Belles, Ferdinand, and his Bull
Inthe Heather (who seemed in that light whiter
than any roan — not wholly there).
You are here, in July's hell, a leafy underworld extruding
from asphalt pores. If the future
Belongs to crowds, their exit is orderly. Sunflower heads
shine greenly and
Truckle to a fine and steady rain. Overall it is cooler
than wished for. The giant ash
Tree that loomed over the alley for a century, there
this morning, is dismantled
Before dusk. Muzzy star, this is my chainsaw
serenade. Muzzy star,

All of my uncles' shade trees are dead. Muzzy star, the third
　　　　rhyme's not much of a charm.
A blimp motors overhead. Summer demands we part
　　　　ways by a fountain.
The spilling water rushes so many leaves, coins, feathers,
　　　　kisses with it, I hadn't thought so many.
One is surrounded soon enough by others, a few of them new
　　　　or less familiar, but mostly
It's the same faces all the time around here. Not necessarily
　　　　a bad thing, if you can forget
That these fragments, too, are dead, their music having
　　　　played late into night. An ambiguous
Surrender awaits our moment. The unwary
　　　　are never unwary enough.

Margaret are you leaving, it takes a po-faced Apollo to squeeze one o'six from the sign outside Community Bank and to mean not Chicago-time but Fahrenheit wouldn't everyone feel cooler if we simply changed our colors and said "it's forty-one degrees Celsius" yes, there would be a period of confusion, but haven't cooler winds always been confused with golden groves the instant first folio changes course and tumbles like a die over the horizon, come back Leif Erikson we are all dreaming your shade, multiplying ephemeral dementia with several iced teas half way to boiling point / then blue October / en route to say goodbye

haunts a bowl haloed by fruit flies,
wedges of darkness are interior
to its secret
curving rescissions
and negative spaces. Books
on the table hoard their history of
gazes.
                                        With reanimated fluency
each one passes through
this, their dialectics mouthed by
moon and star, a visible narration
leaving such compounded
impressions the sleeper
wakes to repeat them as spaces
worn into a canvas of paper

WORSENING SITUATION

un seul trajet à plusieurs voies
— Jacques Derrida (What Is Poetry?)

Jets scratch the sky
In the corner of a boarder's
Window. His face there
Seeks a star through
Its own sigh. Past is passed. The new year
Revives its elder's watery distance. Engendered there,
Everything learns to lean on difference.
The future is unwritten — before or after — evitative,
Deified, as anterior as words that read the same forward
And backward. We could bicker over which is *us*
Heralded in italics, but truth is we'd never know it,
Slouched forth in the manner of a cat
Cleaning itself of all but its shadow.
H E A V E N
Is concrete as the eye saccades across it. Read
On the wing, it takes you momentarily from self
To the abstract of your abandon and so lulls you from
Falling. The cabin creased by sunset,
You are the host floating, an invisible tossing wave
In the middle of the ocean.
A housefly inhabits Versailles.
Having come as tourists, we
Are subject to its weird encroachment.
In the alcoves
so many interesting faces lurk.
Back home, my wife's just inherited some faux pearls
Cradled in a very convincing case: It clicks open
As if they were all that is the world.

A shadow falls on paper   JEWEL   A
living sign

patterns the tongue   Outside it is
snowing   That is   Outside along the
pink shore   Dan, in the future you also
hear the swimmer in your ear speak
'I am safe if not fool enough'
into himself at last

The Fox

knows many things

the Little Des Plaines, Salt Creek

& (all parenthetical waters)

to emeyesseyesseye

What is their substance, whereof are they made,
That millions of strange shadows on them tend?

(The April sky makes bright their cold charade
And spring is a mad Glandelinian.)

No room in the archive —

Catbirds and Killdeers
On telephone wires in great numbers

advertising executives, hotel workers, hospital billings, architects, flight attendants, library catalogues, biotech engineers, hairdressers, armaments consultants, line managers, checks that have cleared, P.R. execs, publishers, taxi drivers, home health-care aides, customer correspondence, cinematographers, security guards, energy consultants, court decisions, subscriber lists

submitted
in familiar print
now strange

a face

bearded

by the shock of never knowing it so
when you were invested   Apostates

and apostles come out of this drawer
what can I do

the spade of one's hand plunged
into files
guarded by dust   Guided
by the annual reported in
no discernible star

cell towers
in great numbers

AT&T's main switching station
hinges most urgently electric
a power with supercomputers

with it I'm on

a prepositional switch into

The slashing
minutes

ceiling adrift
at different heights and different angles
(under fluorescence
no drawer or space to contain
each superfluity)

The fractional state of the
annals   You never brought this
before silence, gathering
things into their causes   Waxing
in the combs of
entries
like "steam sings
thru a kettle"

The / slash /

ing branches

Outside   A game of puzzles inside   He resumed
playing with the map of his fingers
and pried open poems of the late
T'ang   And my heart is a flag
a hundred feet high in the lunar wind   I will
engineer something like it   An eidolon
sun sinking or singing

over the angel I
stunned with a
hand spade   its swim bladder
bad, pinned for two weeks
to the tank's surface

Two sharp blows
and into a waiting hole

except for a few silver
scales

and in three different years he spent
the winter in the same garden
centers of Utah and Texas

Measuring
unnatural wait

POSTAL TELEGRAPH — COMMERCIAL CABLES

Clarence H. MacKay, President

TELEGRAM

DESIGN PATENT NO. 40529

46 ch ad 5 12 32 pm
Hartford Conn. May 22, 16

I was born in Reading, Pennsylvania, am thirty-five years old, a lawyer. My biography is, necessarily, very brief; for I have published nothing.

It seems among the world's best fairy tales

Even if it should cost her
her life, the maiden was determined
to free her brother: "Will you give him to me?" says
the hen-wife
Billy's bull killed the other and drank
his blood   though they fought
long
where you wouldn't know night from day
over hills and sheepwalks
ox trails the Cove of Cork   and old Tom Fox
with his bugle

following my gossip

about death

The coin of Congress,
the kilowatt, is balking

the agency has begun
browning out San Franciso,

"thus as a landscape
it's beautiful," she said.

"I keep coming back
to the same thought:

If completely inauthentic, then
who would make such a

compelling fictitious archive?"

Catalogue #159 GREY GOOSE: gray/tan cardboard, cut and folded, punched, stitched and tied with thin and thick white string, soot-and-spit stick-applied-lines and wiped soot wash.

On a chase
for keys
hidden in a
recipe box

a corner office

'Peter's principle' taped to lid:
certainty only in
misunderstanding

mare's tails brushed
on the winter sky over
a fast track   Express lanes
seen from the 20th floor
where you are sorting

having been shown
the office

flair for technique, flair for indices,
inflections of the *ubi sunt*
having been shown

'chance and chance and thereby starlit'

903 East College
Iowa City, Iowa 52240
25 January 1989

Dear Chris:

There is no question that you delight in words, but I have schooled myself out of such (delicate) pleasures as your poetry affords. I recall — though the context is different — Thoreau's exasperated injunction to Emerson: "Cease this waltz of inspiration." Too much, I find, belongs to subjectivity and sensibility; not enough attention to the things of the world, not enough direct speech (as Williams says, speak what comes off the tongue straight/naturally). How much, on balance, have you to say, to tell us?

In "As it appeared," I doubt that the wheel tilted "superbly," all the more so because of the skill of the juncture that calls attention to it. In "Isolation of the actual," I find "decked" improper in respect to "smell." In "As if it were removal," say it directly: the girls under the umbrellas understand the impingement.

Go back to DISCRETE SERIES and see what Oppen was trying to get on paper at your age.

Ever,
Sherman —

Writing from Mexico
hard to supply return post
for Harriet
And who would see from the
under arm of T / a red globe
constructing objective experience?

No matter how cold the day
Or penetrating the wind
comes a swift moment

where did they go, whoever filed
'No university would support such a
man' in touch with superiors at the U
of New Mexico, 1969   2006
december 1st got cold and snowed
(december 5th even colder)
sidewalks moguled
slick where passers have trudged
in neatly random patterns

            starlit

located in a strong sense
of being without
                  WE ARE RELOCATING

                  The piped-in mall music
A juniper terrace (no loitering in your
little boy's haircut)

One octave higher and the city
cradled in cement
rocked on both sides of a cent-
ury

Wheeling

on one
the VU asked 'Who loves the sun?'
::

UV as performative, as piped-in muse
Yet also expressed as a sense of without
which translates into a seam

on the boundary of any line

pierced by the zed-arrow
'always about to arrive'   as the infinite treble
trembles
& bass bulges through bas-relief
back-masking such urgent distinctions, such music

Buried the silver dollar
this afternoon to left of
stump in garden

Where does lamplight cease to nick it? Here's hot water. Here's hot cider and donut crumbs. Here's the wake of a bread truck. Morning crawls out of silver puddles. Pffff, much of it dust.

★ ★ ★

The green edge of yesterday has said all it could in fervent September grass behind the Episcopal church. *White haired, stinking, cross eyed, stammer tongued, mucous faced* — James Wall, pissing on the toolshed — *best to blush and out with it.* Biking down Spruce Lane, I saw the stark cross stab at wisps of stratus.

★ ★ ★

The tobacco spit of grasshoppers smears the palm. The journey to school is a long one. *The words of the thing twang and twitter. Black they were: branches which have lain in a fog which now a wind is blowing away,* mercury squeezed high and *it's hard to tell loss from gain anyway.* In a garage, sled blades are rusting.

★ ★ ★

The kids have broken the wagon again, climbing in all at once. Let them dangle, or *hide their smiles among the tall glasses in the cupboard, come back when you think the trick's done and you'll find only dead flies there.* Here is where the dismount comes, the against-the-grain contortion, the sudden splash like wave crashed on rock, the exhortation of a tossed bouquet. Falling is that way.

★ ★ ★

And what of 903 College and the old rain gutter still grooved through the single-car driveway cement? Wooded along the ravine, clear contrail in the Googled sky. *Waking is a little hand brushing away dreams. The house becomes a wine that has drugged them out of their senses.* If these chips of paint should burn, if these lowly evergreens should bleed in the dusk…

★ ★ ★

Rough hands and their fat shadows *make logic a butterfly.* Magnificent, in this light, against the white page. And yet there are guests who do not stay.

And the archive opens
on a dark gymnasium
named for the Reverend's
mother 'Loretta
Hall' my only
light a Pepsi machine

lit

place to put change where
it fits Wrapped by F & S
'it' and its 'friends' stood
like shipwrecked men
on a raft whose seats
were made of

Giorgio-de-Chirico
red velvet   Underground
my silver dollar still   A
'breadbasket on a sideboard
where the sun falls'   Machinery
flashing lights
in the temporal lobe   An arrow
stuck in a salt hay bale   Cornstalks
propped on seasonal suburban
porches   The international
harvester falling
from A to B to B to A

eager to be sighted although unborn
the light is the light is the light is the light
and what if in it we costume private
id schemes, ballades to take our place's form
in eyes, witnesses, invisibly torn
like strings of rain across an infant sight;
and we are seven now and undress in light's
sincerity for nothing certain... terms
like racks of spices tumble senses down
the aisle, six become one-fifth, or five
as fifth within a sixth, the numbers live
in posters, prices, carts drawn around
the ends of aisles, eager to be sighted
withal: the bubble's inflated. All are elated

(Of course the Warhol
acetate will enter eBay ritually severed
from its less-than-a-dollar sign (found at a yard
sale behind a water-stained Modern Lovers))

What else

would you put inside
the poem of your
livelihood
as keeps apace beside
you? Perdured in hand
perduring

I had a horse Lord
adored and tortured

The "the" biting / its tail / gulls pick at bones
A shadow falls on paper

as part of the campaign

against the horrors of beauty

whose course the record courses
whose course the inkjet's arrow flies
& traces its arc
into the hive

Chris Glomski was born in Pueblo, Colorado and grew up in Elk Grove Village, Illinois, just northwest of Chicago. He resided in Pisa, Italy from 1991 to 1992, earning a living as a free-lance English teacher.

He currently teaches in the English department at the University of Illinois at Chicago and lives in Humboldt Park.

§

THE NINETEENTH CENTURY AND OTHER POEMS

WAS PRINTED IN AN EDITION OF 250 COPIES

BY MCNAUGHTON & GUNN